# Artists Through the Ages

# Winslow Homer

## Alix Wood

## WINDMILL BOOKS

New York

Published in 2016 by **Windmill Books**, An Imprint of Rosen Publishing
29 East 21ˢᵗ Street, New York, NY 10010

Adaptations to North American edition © 2016 Windmill Books,
An Imprint of Rosen Publishing

Editor for Alix Wood Books: Eloise Macgregor
Designer:  Alix Wood

Photo Credits: Cover, 1 *Portrait of Winslow Homer* by Frank Duveneck
© Christie's; 4 bottom © Dollar Photo Club; 5 top, 15 © nga/ Collection
of Mr. and Mrs. Paul Mellon; 6-7, 12-13, 24-25 © Metropolitan Museum
of Art; 8-9 © Clark Art Institute; 10 © North Carolina Museum of Art;
11 top © Art Renewal Center; 11 bottom, 17 top, 17 bottom, 19, 26,
27 © Museum of Fine Arts, Boston; 14 © nga/W.L. and May T. Mellon
Foundation; 16 © Musée d'Orsay; 18 © Philadelphia Museum of Art;
20 © Terra Museum of American Art; 21, 22 © nga/Ruth K. Henschel/
Charles R. Henschel;  23 © Pennsylvania Academy of Fine Arts; 28, 29
top © Avalon Foundation; 29 bottom © Magic Piano

**Cataloging-in-Publication Data**
Wood, Alix.
Winslow Homer / by Alix Wood.
p. cm. — (Artists through the ages)
Includes index.
ISBN 978-1-4777-5601-0 (pbk.)
ISBN 978-1-4777-5600-3 (6 pack)
ISBN 978-1-4777-5524-2 (library binding)
1. Homer, Winslow, — 1836-1910 — Juvenile literature.
2. Painters — United States — Biography — Juvenile literature.
I. Title.
ND237.H7 W66 2016
759.13—d23

Manufactured in the United States of America
CPSIA Compliance Information: Batch #WS15WM:
For Further Information contact Windmill Books, New York, New York at 1-866-478-0556

# Contents

# Who Was Homer?

The American artist Winslow Homer is probably best known for painting the sea. Born in Boston, Massachusetts, in 1836, he was the second of three sons. His father was a businessman and his mother liked to paint.

Map of the World

North America

Europe

Asia

Africa

South America

Australia

North America · Boston

United States → Massachusetts

Boston Wharf as it is today. The sea inspired young Homer.

Homer grew up in Cambridge, Massachusetts. He spent his childhood playing outside and by the ocean. He loved the countryside and nature. He was good at art from a young age. His mother loved to paint, and taught Homer how to paint using watercolors.

A detail from Homer's 1873 painting *Boys Wading*.

## First Jobs

Homer's father saw an advertisement a printer had put in the local newspaper for "a boy with a talent for drawing." Homer applied, and worked there for two years. He did not like working for other people. He decided to become an **illustrator**-for-hire instead, drawing illustrations for different magazines.

*The Bathers*, an illustration for *Harper's Weekly* magazine, 1873.

# Illustrating War

Homer worked illustrating magazines for almost twenty years. At the same time he went to art classes at the National Academy of Design. Mainly, though, Homer taught himself to paint. His mother wanted him to go to Europe and study painting there.

Instead, one of the magazines Homer worked for sent him to the **front lines** of the American Civil War! His job was to draw battle scenes and life at the front lines for the magazine.

*Prisoners from the Front*, 1866. What are each of the three prisoners on the left feeling, do you think?

Homer painted this oil painting one year after the war ended. It represents an actual scene from the war when Brigadier General Francis Barlow captured several **Confederate** officers. The background shows the battlefield at Petersburg, Virginia.

# A Stay in Paris

In 1867, Homer took a trip to France. His painting, *Prisoners from the Front,* was being **exhibited** in Paris at the time. He spent a year there, sending illustrations of Paris life to *Harper's* magazine back home.

In France, Homer painted **landscapes** of farmworkers when he was not producing his magazine illustrations. When Homer returned from Europe, his style of painting hadn't really been changed by the artists in Paris. Homer had already developed his own style. He wanted to paint American **subjects** in his own way.

*Bridle Path, White Mountains, 1868*

## An American Scene

*Bridle Path, White Mountains* was painted soon after Homer returned home. He chose to paint a very American landscape and subject. Homer often painted women enjoying an outdoors life.

# Country Life

After the American Civil War, people wanted to think about happier times. Homer understood this need for **nostalgia** and his paintings during the 1870s often show children enjoying a happy childhood in the summer sun. They are painted helping on the farm, sailing boats, reading stories, and playing games with their friends.

*Weaning the Calf,* 1875

The Reaper, 1878

# Summertime

Paintings of happy children playing together gave people hope that there would never be another war. The future, in the summer sunshine, was looking bright.

Boys in a Pasture, 1874

# Snap the Whip

Snap the whip is a children's game where children hold hands in a chain. The tail of the chain whips around as the lead children change direction. The boy on the left has flown off with the force of the "whip!"

# The Red Schoolhouse

This one-room red schoolhouse is in many of Homer's paintings. In the 1870s, more and more people were moving to the city and larger city schools. There was a nostalgia about the days of small country schools at that time.

*Snap the Whip*, 1872

# Boys in Boats

*Breezing Up* is probably Homer's best-known painting. He created the painting from **sketches** that he made. It took Homer three years to complete *Breezing Up*. He changed it many times before he was happy. **Infrared** images, which can look under the paint, show there was another boy by the mast, and another boat in the background.

Breezing Up, 1873-1876

# Spot the Difference

Homer painted *The Flirt* before completing *Breezing Up*. Can you can see the fourth boy by the mast in this painting?
The adult is steering the boat as well as holding the sail's rope. Can you see any other differences?
Which painting do you prefer?

The Flirt, 1874

Homer exhibited *Breezing Up* at an important exhibition in Philadelphia, Pennsylvania, in 1876. The exhibition was celebrating 100 years since the signing of the **Declaration of Independence**. Over 10 million people visited the fair, and people liked Homer's painting.

# Time in England

From spring 1881 to November 1882, Homer spent some time in England. He lived at Cullercoats, a small fishing village in the northeast. There was a small community of artists there.

Homer was impressed by the tough lives of the local fisherwomen. Their survival totally relied on the sea. He painted them and their everyday lives, hauling and cleaning the fish, mending the nets, and waiting on the beach for their men to return safe. He used watercolor in these paintings, rather than oil paints.

## The Gleaners

Do you think Homer was influenced by the French painter Jean-François Millet? Millet painted hardworking women, as in this painting below, called *The Gleaners*.

*Girl with Red Stockings,* 1882

*A Fresh Breeze,* around 1881

# Bravery at Sea

Homer moved to Prouts Neck, Maine, in 1883. He was inspired by the bravery of the men who worked at sea there. His painting below shows a rescue using a new device known as a **breeches buoy**. A line is fired from ship to ship, attached, and then the casualty is hauled across above the crashing waves. Homer had seen a demonstration of the device in 1883. Why do you think he painted the scarf flapping over the man's face?

*The Life Line, 1884*

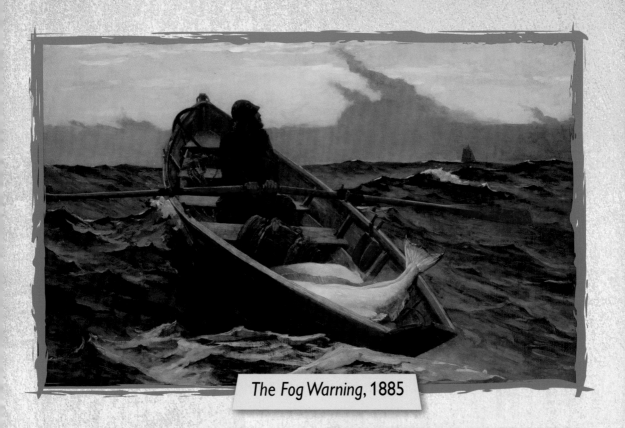

*The Fog Warning*, 1885

In *The Fog Warning*, Homer paints a tense moment at sea. The fisherman has had a successful day. His boat is full of fish, but his day is not over yet. The fog is coming in and he may not reach his ship before he gets lost in the mist.

## Prouts Neck

Homer's family bought some land by the ocean at Prouts Neck, Maine. Homer built a **studio** there in 1883, with a balcony overlooking the ocean. He would have created these paintings there by the sea.

19

# Chasing the Sun

Maine was cold in wintertime. Homer often spent his vacations in Florida, Cuba, and the Bahamas. He traded the dark, Atlantic water for the sparkling, turquoise Caribbean Sea.

Homer was sent to Nassau in the Bahamas to create some illustrations for *Century Magazine*. Nassau was a popular tourist destination. Homer painted the scenery and island life.

*A Garden in Nassau,* 1885

*Salt Kettle, Bermuda*, 1885

# Watercolors

Homer used watercolor in these paintings. He often left parts of the white paper showing through. The brilliant white looked like the bright sunlight. His paintings look bright and happy compared to the gray skies of Cullercoats.

Salt Kettle is a bay in Bermuda where salt was unloaded from the boats. Homer painted this picture from a guesthouse that overlooks the bay.

# Hunter and Hunted

Homer's watercolor *On the Trail* shows a hunter with his hounds in a forest. Homer enjoyed hunting and fishing and loved being outdoors. You can sense the tense excitement of the man and his dogs, even though you can't see what they are hunting. Do you think the painting would be better if Homer had put a deer in it? Or would that spoil the excitement of the hunt?

*On the Trail, 1892*

# Painting from Death!

It's called "painting from life" when artists use a live model as a **reference** for their work. In *The Fox Hunt*, below, Homer used a dead fox and some dead crows, propped up in the snow using sticks and string! At first the crows didn't look very good. He threw some corn outside and sketched some living ones that came to eat the corn, instead.

*The Fox Hunt*, 1893

The crows look like a dark, scary cloud above the fox. A fox is normally the hunter, but in this painting the crows are attacking him.

# The Gulf Stream

The Gulf Stream is a strong ocean current that starts at the tip of Florida. Homer crossed the Gulf Stream several times on journeys to Florida and the Caribbean. Its power fascinated him. He painted several pictures of wrecked boats with sharks circling them.

## A Popular Painting!

Homer's *The Gulf Stream* was exhibited at the National Academy of Design in 1906. All the members of the academy's jury wrote to the Metropolitan Museum of Art asking that they buy the painting, which they did.

*The Gulf Stream,* 1899

The sailor in *The Gulf Stream* seems to be ignoring the sharks, the **waterspout**, and the ship behind him. Perhaps he has given up hope, or maybe he's seen a rescue boat off to the right? What do you think?

# Wilderness

Homer liked to vacation in the Adirondacks. The area was a wilderness then, in the mountains of New York State. Homer created more than a hundred paintings from his many visits to the area between 1870 and 1910. Many images were of hunting scenes, or of the local guides who would show visitors the best spots to hunt game.

*Hudson River, 1892*

The Adirondack Guide, 1894

# The Adirondack Guide

Homer painted several watercolors of the same Adirondack guide, thought to be Rufus Wallace. The guides were happy to pose as models, unlike Homer's fellow hunters. The guides were also like a part of the wilderness to Homer.

# Homer's Last Years

Homer suffered a mild stroke in his later life. He had difficulty speaking and controlling his muscles. He never completely recovered, but he continued to work. Having never married or had children, work was his main focus.

One of his last paintings, *Right and Left* (opposite), is thought to be one of his best. He wrote to his brother saying he was working on a "most surprising picture." "Right" and "left" probably refers to the two barrels of a gun.

## You Decide!

When you look at the painting, you are not sure if both the ducks have been shot, or if they have escaped. Did Homer paint them at the top of the paper so they have space to fall down into it? Or will they escape the picture and fly away?

You can just see the hunter by the left-hand duck's leg.

*Right and Left, 1909*

Homer died quietly in his Prouts Neck studio in 1910. Although he was a leading American painter making a living from his work, he only really became well-known after his death. The Portland Museum of Art bought Homer's studio in Prouts Neck and opened it to the public in 2012.

*Homer's studio at Prouts Neck, Maine. It is now a museum.*

# Glossary

**breeches buoy**
(BREE-chez BOO-ee)
A device which can be used to hold and transfer a passenger to safety from a ship.

**Confederate**
(kun-FEH-duh-ret)
A person who fought for the South in the Civil War.

**Declaration of Independence**
(deh-kluh-RAY-shun UV in-duh-PEN-dints)
An official announcement signed on July 4, 1776, in which American colonists stated they were free of British rule.

**exhibited** (ek-ZIH-bit-ed)
Shown in public for people to see.

**front lines**
(FRUNT LYNZ)
The troops at the front of the battle.

**illustrator**
(IH-lus-tray-ter)
A person who draws or paints pictures that go with a story.

**infrared** (in-fruh-RED)
Light waves that we can't see because they are beyond the color red in the visible light range.

**landscapes**
(LAND-skaypz)
Pictures of the natural scenery.

**nostalgia**
(nuh-STAL-juh)
A longing or affection for a period in the past.

**reference** (REH-frens)
A source of information.

**sketches** (SKECH-ez)
Quick drawings.

**studio** (STOO-dee-oh)
A room or building where an artist works.

**subjects** (SUB-jekts)
The people or things that are being painted.

**waterspout**
(WAH-ter-spowt)
A tornado that happens over a lake or ocean.

# Websites

For web resources related to the subject of this book, go to: **www.windmillbooks.com/weblinks** and select this book's title.

# Read More

Alexander, Heather. *A Child's Introduction to Art*. New York: Black Dog and Leventhal Publishers, 2014.

National Gallery of Art. *Winslow Homer Coloring Book*. Oregon: Pomegranate, 2009.

Venezia, Mark. *Winslow Homer* (Getting to Know the World's Greatest Artists). New York: Children's Press, 2004.

# Index